1st Edition
MoneySeeds
30 Day Wealth Building Devotional

AUTHOR
Christopher Brown
FaithFinance, Inc
www.faithfinance.org
chrisb@faithfinance.org
562.572.7793

Published by
FaithFinance using
Blurb Book Wright Software

Copyright 2020 by Christopher Brown and FaithFinance, Inc all rights reserved.

No part of this publication may be reproduce, stored in a retrieval system or transmitted in any way by any means, electronic, mechanical, photocopy, recording or otherwise without the prior written permission of the author except as provided by USA copyright law

Blurb provided layout designs and graphic elements and are copyright Blurb, Inc 2020. The book author retains sole copyright to his contributions to this book.

The verses in this book have been translated using the English Standard Version (ESV)

Published in the United States of America
Paperback version
ISBN: **978-1-7345500-0-9**
1. Religion / Christian life
2. Religion & Spirituality
3. Personal Finance

DEDICATION

This devotional book is dedicated to my all of my fellow brothers and sisters in Christ. Time with Jehovah and time in His Word is food for our souls.

Your word is a lamp to my feet
and a light to my path.
Psalm 119:105

SPECIAL ACKNOWLEDGEMENTS

I would like to thank my wife Allison, my son Tyre and my daughter Christina for their support and critique of this book. Also, the FaithFinance community who offered input into the cover design selection process.

Table of Contents

Forward 5

WEEK 1
DAY 1 - Deuteronomy 28:15 7
DAY 2 - Deuteronomy 8:18 9
DAY 3 - Psalms 24:1 11
DAY 4 - Psalms 35:27 13
DAY 5 - Psalms 112:3 15
DAY 6 - Proverbs 10:22 17
DAY 7 - Proverbs 11:15 19

WEEK 2
DAY 8 - Proverbs 13:22 21
DAY 9 - Proverbs 13:11 23
DAY 10 - Proverbs 17:18 25
DAY 11 - Proverbs 19:21 27
DAY 12 - Proverbs 20:4 29
DAY 13 - Proverbs 21:20 31
DAY 14 - Proverbs 22:7 33
DAY 15 - Proverbs 24:30-34 35

WEEK 3
DAY 16 - Proverbs 29:18 37
DAY 17 - Ecclesiastes 5:5 39
DAY 18 - Ecclesiastes 11:2 41
DAY 19 - Matthew 6:33 43
DAY 20 - Matthew 6:19-21 45
DAY 21 - Matthew 6:24 47
DAY 22 - Matthew 25:14-30 49

WEEK 4
DAY 23 - Luke 14:28 51
DAY 24 - Luke 16:11 53
DAY 25 - John 10:10 55
DAY 26 - John 15:5 57
DAY 27 - Romans 13:8 59
DAY 28 - 2 Corinthians 8:9 61
DAY 29 - 1 Timothy 5:8 63
DAY 30 - 1 Timothy 6:17 65

Author's Bio 66

FORWARD

We are all looking for either "seeds of knowledge" or "little nuggets of wisdom" that will help us make prudent decisions when it comes to our personal finances. Even though there are many different devotional books available on the topic of personal finance, I have not seen a devotional book focused on the topic wealth building. So felt lead to create something which could help fill the void.

The Bible has a lot to say about money, wealth (abundance), wealth building, greed, contentment and a variety of other topics as they pertain to our financial and spiritual lives. Over the years, I've heard it said more than once that the Bible has well over 2000 verses about money. Clearly, the topic of personal finances is important to Jehovah and His Word offers us instructions on how to be good stewards, tithing and more importantly how the love of money can influence our character.

People turn to devotional books for various reasons. Some to meet a deep spiritual need or to have intimacy with God, others to find comfort or to seek wisdom from the Word. Whatever your personal reason is, my desire is that you find inspiration, wisdom and empowerment from the pages that follow. As a community of believers, we all are on this spiritual journey of learning how to live faithfully, so we can live abundantly.

There are a few opinions on how long it takes for someone to form a new habit. One is called the 21/90 Rule. The rule is simple enough. Commit to a personal goal for 21 straight days. After three weeks, the goal should have become a habit. Once you have established the habit, repeat it for another 90 days to lock it in. Hence, the format of this 30 Day Wealth Building Devotional. The idea is for you to take one month to renew your mind in God's Word, then re-read the devotional two or three more times to discover new revelations and "lock in" the principles as your year progresses.

Deuteronomy

DAY 1 - Deuteronomy 28:12

The Lord will open to you his good treasury, the heavens, to give the rain to your land in its season and to bless all the work of your hands. And you shall lend to many nations, but you shall not borrow.

Meditation -

So often we all see wealth building as something WE do. While it does take intention and effort on our parts, we must not forget who truly owns the "treasures" we so diligently seek. Jehovah's is the owner of "good treasures" and He is the one who gives out what He owns. The truth which stands out most in this verse is Jehovah's intention for His children to be the financial leaders in this world. His intention is that WE are to be the ones controlling the world's wealth and resources. Obviously, He wants to bless us, but more importantly He wants bless others. As wealth builders we all have this wonderful opportunity to lead and be a vessel of Jehovah's blessing to others.

For those of us who feel we have never attained this position, the question is what do we need to change in our lives so that we do? For those who feel they have, the question would be are we using our position of influence to glorify Jehovah and to bless others.

What treasures has Jehovah provided you?

Action Plan -

Goal - How can you use your treasures to serve others?

Why is this important to me?

What do I need to do to achieve my goal?

When is my deadline?

DAY 2 - Deuteronomy 8:18

You shall remember the Lord your God, for it is he who gives you power to get wealth, that he may confirm his covenant that he swore to your fathers, as it is this day.

Meditation -

This verse directly challenges our sense of personal pride. Regardless of culture, we all want to believe WE are the masters of our own destiny when it comes to financial achievements. Success gurus always proclaim the gospel of self-actualization and encourage us to "take control" because the power to achieve is within us. However, this verse states something different by making the claim "Yahweh" has the power and that His power is graciously given to us.

Moses directs us to the duty of a prosperous condition by reminding us to always remember our Benefactor. In everything, we must give thanks and arm ourselves against the temptations of being in a prosperous condition. Mainly the temptation to pride. Forgetfulness of Jehovah, and carnal-mindedness can become very strong when we have financial success. The great secret of Divine Providence, of infinite wisdom and goodness is that these are the resources to all the changes and trials believers experience. Nothing can render an outward and inward trial more effectual, but the power of the Spirit of God. Jehovah's giving and our getting are reconciled in our spiritual wealth.

The Hebrew word used for "wealth" means strength, efficiency and wealth. The point I see is that the power being offered is for more than just gaining financial wealth. It is a power to obtain abundant living in many areas of life. Wealth building is not just about money, but a more holistic approach towards life.

Action Plan -

Goal - What power or ability do you need from Jehovah?

Why is this important to me?

What do I need to do to achieve my goal?

When is my deadline?

Psalms

DAY 3 - Psalm 24:1

A Psalm of David. The earth is the Lord's and the fullness thereof, the world and those who dwell therein,

Meditation -

Who really owns what? David begins with a representation of God's dominion over this world in general, and his providential presence in every part of it. This verse strongly states that ALL the creatures of this world are the Lord's, and especially the inhabitants wherewith the earth is replenished. This means we ourselves are not our own, a concept which is really hard at times to conceive. To think that our bodies and our souls are owned by Jehovah just does not sit well with our desire for autonomy. Since this is true, think of the implications when it comes to who owns our possessions. When we think of "wealth building" a few questions come up.

1. Purpose – Why are we building wealth?
2. Legacy - For whom are we building it?
3. Control – Who really is determining or controlling the outcome of our success?
4. Ownership - Since Jehovah is the owner of all, what are you?

Action Plan -

Goal - What are your answers to the four questions above?

Why are they important to me?

What do I need to do to achieve my goals?

When is my deadline?

DAY 4 - Psalm 35:27

Let those who delight in my righteousness shout for joy and be glad and say evermore, "Great is the Lord, who delights in the welfare of his servant!"

Meditation -

I was recently waiting to be seated in a restaurant and this little 5-year-old boy was so cute. While the adults were patiently waiting, listening to the holiday music in the background this young man seized the moment! Without a care in the world he was dancing his little heart away. Securely standing by his mother's side he was bouncing up and down to the holiday beats as though this was his stage and we were his audience. The innocence of youth really knows how to express feelings in our hearts when we are full of joy.

This verse speaks directly to some of the relationship dynamics we have with Jehovah. For those of us who genuinely delight or "take pleasure in" His righteousness, we should be experiencing and expressing joy. When we focus on Jehovah's character, we are poised to understand that Jehovah equally delights in our overall success in life. The Hebrew word to focus on here is "Shalom", which in this context could be defined as completeness, soundness, welfare or peace. In some translations the word prosperity is used.

We would not initially think that the posture of our heart is important to our wealth building efforts. The concept in the verse clearly expands beyond our financial wellbeing and into our lives holistically. To the extent our monetary building endeavors are in alignment with His purposes we should expect His delightful endorsement.

Action Plan -

Goal - What is the posture of my heart towards God's righteousness?

Why is this important to me?

What do I need to do to adjust my heart?

When is my deadline?

DAY 5 - Psalm 112:3

Wealth and riches are in his house, and his righteousness endures forever.

Meditation -
If you have never been to the Palace of Versailles it is worth the trip. The French Baroque style of architecture is typically executed in pure opulence and this luxurious mansion is no exception. The large halls, corridors and chamber rooms are lined with gold and magnificent works of art. At one point in history the palace furniture was made out of pure silver, 20 tons to be exact.

Even though Versailles is breathtaking and an architectural masterpiece, it was made by man. It is nothing in comparison to the house of Jehovah. The general theme which runs through Psalm 112 is the comparison of the godly man to Jehovah. The point is simple, as we assume Jehovah's character and live out those attributes we will receive the blessings associated with them. A couple of these blessings are wealth and riches. This is a promise which has been given to multiple generations.

I am not preaching a "prosperity gospel", never will. However, wealth building is an authentic part of the fruit we can expect to see in a believer's life. Our responsibility in this equation is to take pleasure in Jehovah and His ways of living life and building wealth.

Action Plan -
Goal - Are wealth and riches are to part of my house?

Why is this important to me?

What do I need to do to achieve my goal?

When is my deadline?

Proverbs

DAY 6 - [Proverbs 10:22](#)

The blessing of the Lord makes rich, and he adds no sorrow with it.

Meditation -

So many of us experience stress while trying to provide for the financial needs of our family. Whether it is spending hours commuting to and from work, dealing with corporate politics, ungrateful clients, unrealistic project schedules and workloads or demanding bosses. We all have stories of stressful workdays.

One of the blessings Jehovah gives us is peace or calm while we work to meet our financial obligations. It is wealth building with little stress or as stated "no sorrow." This should cause us pause if we are experiencing much distress in our pursuit to provide the financial needs of our family. I am not negating, that there will be hard times and challenges. We can expect those, however, in the challenges we should also expect to experience a sense of Jehovah's peace. This is the peace which goes beyond simply having a positive attitude. It is the peace which comforts the depths of our souls and spirit. As the picture illustrates, it is a peace which understands that there is always a better tomorrow because Jehovah is involved. I admit that I am not there every day, but at least I can see the target.

Action Plan -

Goal - Are my wealth building endeavors accompanied by peace?

Why is this important to me?

What do I need to do to achieve my goal?

When is my deadline?

DAY 7 - Proverbs 11:15

Whoever puts up security for a stranger will surely suffer harm, but he who hates striking hands in pledge is secure.

Meditation -
Simply put, DO NOT BE A BANK for someone you do not know!! This is a clear warning regarding the perils of assuming the debt or financial responsibilities of someone else. Especially if we do not know their character.

Surely, we should not jeopardize the welfare of our families, our own peace or our ability to meet our financial responsibilities by assuming the debt responsibility of others. It is not wise if we associate or do business deals with those who do not know how to wisely manage their own finances. These associations at the very least will not assist us in our wealth building efforts. More importantly, they could be very harmful beyond our finances and impact other areas of our lives.

Action Plan -
Goal:

Why is this important to me?

What do I need to do to achieve my goal?

When is my deadline?

DAY 8 - Proverbs 13:22

A good man leaves an inheritance to his children's children, but the sinner's wealth is laid up for the righteous.

Meditation -

These are striking words which leave no room for ambiguous interpretation. They give us a picture of the millions and billions of dollars controlled by those who choose to pursue a lifestyle of unrighteousness. This thought challenges us to think about what kind of financial legacy we are preparing to leave the succeeding generations. The path which is in opposition to Jehovah's directions will eventually result in the loss of whatever material possessions this person has acquired in this life. The interesting twist is that in the end this person's wealth will eventually wind up in the possession of God's people.

I will admit that sometimes I wonder. However, the verse promises for those who chose God's path, they are empowered to acquire wealth which will impact at least two generations after them. Therefore, the "good man" will have a financial legacy his grand children can build upon.

Action Plan -

Goal - Could you be considered the "good man or woman" illustrated?

Why is this important to me?

What do I need to do to achieve my goal?

When is my deadline?

DAY 9 - Proverbs 13:11

Wealth gained hastily will dwindle, but whoever gathers little by little will increase it.

Meditation -
The text in the original Hebrew is direct about the right methods for obtaining wealth. The text implies three things:

I. THAT WEALTH IN ITSELF IS A GOOD THING.
1. All men strive for it, in obedience to the original command — to possess the earth and subdue it.
2. The services it can render are evidences of its value.
3. The Word of God approves it. Not money, but the "love" of it, is "a root of evil."

II. WEALTH MAY BE OBTAINED IN TWO DIFFERENT WAYS.
1. The way of vanity, which may represent fraud, gambling, reckless speculation, etc.
2. The way of diligent and steady labor.

III. THE INCREASE OR DECREASE OF WEALTH IS AFFECTED BY THE MODE OF ITS ACQUSITION.
1. Wealth acquired by vanity or fraudulent means is not highly appreciated and its value is not understood; hence, it is usually quickly spent.
2. The converse, wealth acquired with hard work is highly appreciated. As a result, it is handled with wisdom and will over time increase.

In other words, when it comes to wealth building, the tortoise had the right idea. Do not be distracted by others actions, but stay focused on your finish line and be determined to cross it. Be steady and consistent daily with small progressive steps forward towards your goal.

Action Plan -
Goal - What are your wealth building goals?
Why is this important to me?

What daily steps do I need to consistently do to achieve my goal?
When is my deadline?

DAY 10 - Proverbs 17:18

One who lacks sense gives a pledge and puts up security in the presence of his neighbor.

Meditation -
DO NOT ASSUME THE DEBT OF SOMEONE YOU DO KNOW!!
Have you ever secured a loan for a family member or friend. How did it turn out? I am sure for some things worked out okay, but for others not so much. A lack of financial wisdom in this area can be costly. An unwise person will assume the debt of another. This is a risky proposition which is done in our culture all the time, especially in the area of consumer borrowing. The risk is clear, they default, you pay. The cost to you is that the financial needs of your family are postponed. Until the debt is paid, your wealth building plans will also be postponed.

This is genuinely a MoneySeed of wisdom. This verse is stating what is wise. People close to you or even your own feelings may try and persuade you to not follow this principle. Do not listen.

Action Plan -
Goal - What this principle trying to teach me?

Why is this important to me?

What do I need to do to fully understand the lesson?

When is my deadline?

DAY 11 - Proverbs 19:21

Many are the plans in the mind of a man, but it is the purpose of the Lord that will stand.

Meditation -
When it comes to financial goals we all have dreams and desires which we make plans to accomplish. For some, it is material, the house, a car or apple stock. For others, it is the ability to support a cause or some philanthropic endeavor. Only those directed by Jehovah will endure the test of time. Again, if our dreams and desires to build wealth are void of Divine purpose there is a strong possibility that they may not come to pass. Even if they do, they may not bear the fruit we desire or have the lasting impact we had hoped for. However, for those wealth building plans which are rooted in Divine purpose we are promised that they will reap the benefits of Divine principles.

Action Plan -
Goal - Do my wealth building plans of Divine purpose:

Why is this important to me?

What do I need to do to achieve my goal?

When is my deadline?

DAY 12 - Proverbs 20:4

The sluggard does not plow in the autumn; he will seek at harvest and have nothing.

Meditation -

The truth in this Proverb has both spiritual and carnal lessons. In the spiritual, the idle man is unseasonable in his repose, and equally unseasonable in his expectation. In the formation of our character, nothing will come to us which is noble or elevating, unless it is sought with intention and diligence.

In the carnal world, farmers live this truth every day. Even those of us who are urban farmers know that if we don't work our little backyard gardens in the autumn months that there will not be a harvest come summer. Jehovah's wealth building economy is built on the principle of sow now and reap later.

Action Plan -

Goal - What do I need to be doing now, to reap benefits later?

Why is this important to me?

What do I need to do to achieve my goal?

When is my deadline?

HOME SWEET HOME

DAY 13 - Proverbs 21:20

Precious treasure and oil are in a wise man's dwelling, but a foolish man devours it.

Meditation -

American author and poet, L. Frank Baum, gave us the phrase, " There is no place like Home." in his famed fantasy tale, The Wonderful Wizard of Oz. The fact that the concept of "home" has talismanic power over every human heart is clearly intentional by Divine design. No one can deny the conscious and sub-conscious affects of our early beginnings at home. These embryonic experiences of home-life have molded us into who we are today. Home-life is the seed time for an eternal harvest. God Himself instituted the family relationships as one of His antidotes for Satan's various enticements.

God has designed there to be great treasure spiritually, emotionally, psychologically, physically and materially in our homes. If we are wise, we will see the value of these resources and protect them. As astute stewards we will handle them prudence. In the area of wealth building the result will be that our financial resources will enhance our lives and the lives of generations to come. As for the unwise, well, they will simply enjoy consuming their treasures.

Action Plan -

Goal - What are your precious treasures?

Why is this important to me?

What do I need to do to keep them precious?

When is my deadline?

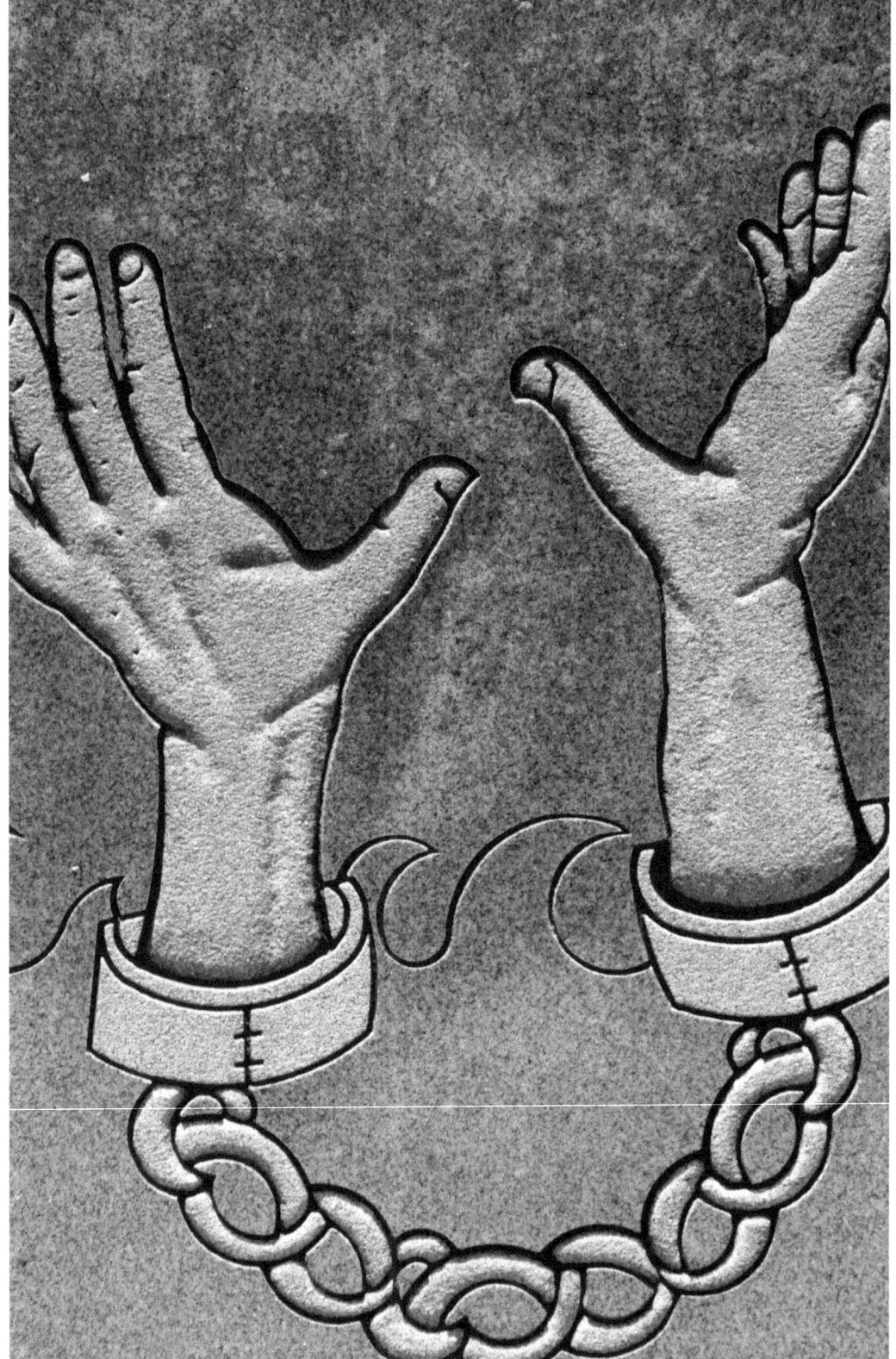

DAY 14 - Proverbs 22:7

The rich rules over the poor, and the borrower is the slave of the lender.

Meditation -

This proverb is so straight forward, even in the original Hebrew. It is direct, there will be those who are rich (wealth builders) and poor. Which category do you want to be in? The verse is blunt, there will be borrowers and lenders (wealth builders). Again, which category do you want to be in? Slavery is never a good option when you have a choice. Who will you choose to be?

Action Plan -

My goals to being a wealth builder:

Why are they important to me?

What do I need to do to achieve my goal?

When is my deadline?

DAY 15 - Proverbs 24:30-34

I passed by the field of a sluggard, by the vineyard of a man lacking sense, and behold, it was all overgrown with thorns; the ground was covered with nettles, and its stone wall was broken down. Then I saw and considered it; I looked and received instruction. A little sleep, a little slumber, a little folding of the hands to rest, and poverty will come upon you like a robber, and want like an armed man.

Meditation -

When I was growing up there was an empty house on my block which was completely overgrown with grass, weeds and shrubs. To us kids, it was known as the "haunted house." Whether it was or not did not matter, to us the lack of care symbolized something negative which brought insecurity and was something which needed to be avoided. I think we all have had a "haunted house" in our childhood past which reflect on a similar story of neglect illustrated in the Proverb.

Our physical world contains the potential for life, beauty, and purpose. However, in order to achieve its Divine design we need to cultivate it. Slothfulness and neglect in all areas of life will result in loss and ruin. This principle is so true in the area of gaining financial freedom and building up assets. One of our goals is to leave a financial legacy to the subsequent generations. When trying to build this legacy if we are lazy, have no plan and are neglectful we will not have much to leave. Our financial house will just be another empty "haunted house."

Action Plan -

Goal - Am I building a financial legacy?

Why is this important to me?

What do I need to do to achieve my goal?

When is my deadline?

DAY 16 - Proverbs 29:18

Where there is no prophetic vision the people cast off restraint, but blessed is he who keeps the law.

Meditation -

There are two parts to this proverb, the first being vision. However, not just any vision, but one that is divine in origin. We can have our visions of success, but what we need is Jehovah's vision of success for us. His visions for us come from a pure place with His supernatural power as the foundation. To achieve our divine destiny we will need to go through some obstacles. In order to get through them we will need power beyond or abilities.

There is the second part. Our prophetic visions of success must be aligned with our desire to be obedient. Sometimes the end of the above verse is translated, "he who keeps wise instruction." With either translation the need of both personal discipline and righteous living are clear. Synergy with Jehovah will yield amazing results in many areas of life, including wealth building. Without it, much time and effort will be wasted.

Action Plan -

Goal - What financial vision has God given me?

Why is this important to me?

What do I need to do to achieve this goal?

When is my deadline?

Ecclesiates

DAY 17 - Ecclesiastes 5:5

It is better that you should not vow than that you should vow and not pay.

Meditation -
Our words and what we say are very important to Jehovah, especially when spoken to Him. King Solomon wants to make the point when you speak to God keep your words few. This principle is applicable when we speak to each other as well. The translation of the phrase "not pay" is the Hebrew word "shalam" meaning to amend, to be complete or restore. When applying this principle to our personal finances clearly, we see the importance of choosing our words and commitments wisely. If and when we need to borrow money there is always the promise we make to pay the lender back. When you borrow, pay it back; if you cannot, then do not borrow.

Action Plan -
Goal:

Why is this important to me?

What do I need to do to achieve my goal?

When is my deadline?

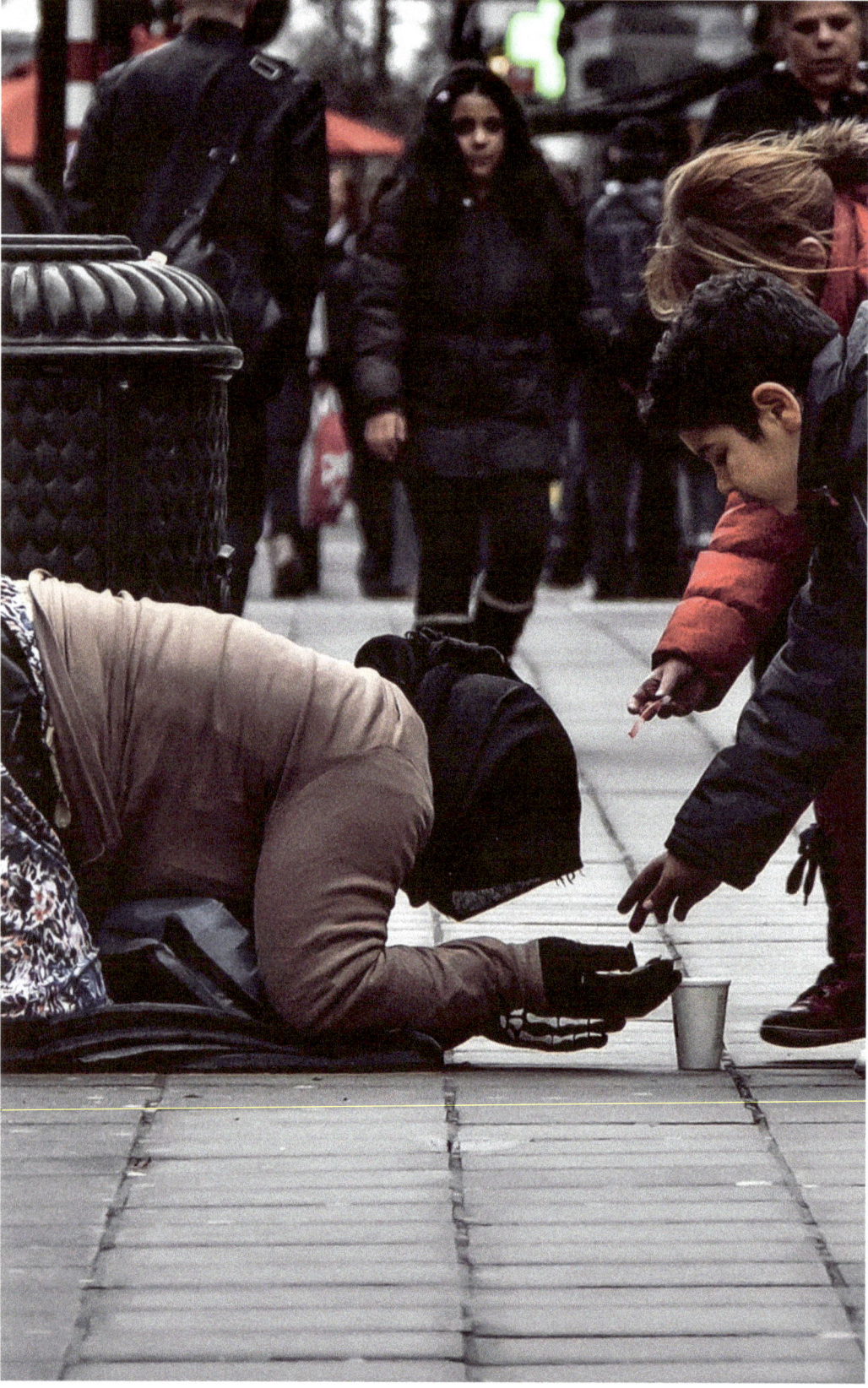

DAY 18 - Ecclesiastes 11:2

Give a portion to seven, or even to eight, for you know not what disaster may happen on earth.

Meditation -
The gift of giving. The author of Ecclesiastes puts his powers of wisdom to work by examining the human experience and the act of charity. Charity is an essential part of the Christian experience. We cannot know or control what will happen to us or others in the future. Therefore, there are times when our efforts remain balanced on the razor's edge of uncertainty.

Giving generously in the present is an act of faithful living. When things in life are prosperous for us, it is important we bless those less fortunate than ourselves. When things are not prosperous, it is even more imperative that we do it. The faithful act of giving is rooted in trust. Who do we trust with our future? Ourselves or Jehovah? Sowing when times are good gives us something to reap when times are uncertain or challenging.

Action Plan -
Goal - Is there money I can give now?

Why is this important to me?

What do I need to do to achieve my goal?

When is my deadline?

Matthew

DAY 19 - Matthew 6:33

But seek first the kingdom of God and his righteousness, and all these things will be added to you.

Meditation -

Having scripture context here is important to fully understanding what this verse is trying to teach us. This is a part of Jesus's Sermon on the Mount in which he warns us about being focused too much on the things of this life. He strongly encourages us not to be anxious for anything. A tough challenge to say in the least. Financial anxiety often ensnares the poor as much as the love of wealth does the rich. The underlining theme of the Sermon on the Mount is the Kingdom of God and that our first pursuit in life shall be seeking it all areas of our daily living.

The point is Jehovah is sovereign and we cannot alter the disposals of Providence. Therefore, we should submit ourselves to it. In our pursuit of His Kingdom we shall seek to live a life of holiness, justice or as stated, righteousness. The foundational issue is we are to seek Jehovah's character, His wise counsel and sovereignty in all material things, including our finances. The promise is that our financial concerns will be addressed by Him in due time. Put another way, if we focus on living right, He will focus on our wealth building success.

Action Plan -

Goal - Is your priority the Kingdom of God?

Why is this important to me?

What do I need to do to achieve my goal?

When is my deadline?

DAY 20 - Matthew 6:19-21

"Do not lay up for yourselves treasures on earth, where moth and rust destroy and where thieves break in and steal, but lay up for yourselves treasures in heaven, where neither moth nor rust destroys and where thieves do not break in and steal. For where your treasure is, there your heart will be also.

Meditation -

Another small excerpt from the Sermon on the Mount which speaks to the motivation of our hearts. During his infamous exhortation on living, Jesus offers us much wisdom and makes a transition from religions actions to more common ones. In these words, he warns us against making earthly possessions a priority. In our quest to build a financial legacy that we can pass on to the next generation it will be challenging for us to keep our priorities in line with Jehovah's. We ALL are susceptible to lure of the things which sparkle and shine. We ALL can become fixated on what is temporary and lose focus on our eternal purpose. As stewards we simply manage the wealth Jehovah has blessed us with. As stated, where our treasure is, so will our hearts be. Jehovah treasures us and His desires is for us to treasure Him.

Action Plan -

Goal - What do you deeply treasure?

Why is this important to me?

What do I need to do to adjust my focus?

When is my deadline?

DAY 21 - Matthew 6:24

"No one can serve two masters, for either he will hate the one and love the other, or he will be devoted to the one and despise the other. You cannot serve God and money.

Meditation -

Money, the last word in this verse is translated in the Greek as "mamonas" or mammon. It literally means wealth, riches, money, possessions or property. Again, Jesus addresses the condition and focus of our hearts. Here, he obviously compares a personification for the sake of contrasting the service or worship of money with that which is due to God. The comparison describes two distinct results of the attempt to combine the two forms of service which are incompatible. We are warned of our human tendency to love one, and a really hate the other.

None us want to believe that in our quest to obtain wealth and the "good life" we will hate the service of God in the inner most depths of our heart. We All need to be careful of such naivety. If we our completely honest with ourselves, our pursuit of financial freedom can consume our minds, hearts, actions and time.

Action Plan -

Goal - Which master am I serving?

Why is this important to me?

What do I need to do to serve the right master?

When is my deadline?

DAY 22 - Matthew 25:14-30

"For it will be like a man going on a journey, who called his servants and entrusted to them his property. To one he gave five talents, to another two, to another one, to each according to his ability. Then he went away. He who had received the five talents went at once and traded with them, and he made five talents more. So also he who had the two talents made two talents more. But he who had received the one talent went and dug in the ground and hid his master's money.

Meditation -

The infamous "talent" parable. Jehovah wants us to be wise and understand the system of wealth creation as He has designed it to function. I believe He wants to literally double the provisions He has provided us if not more. There have been many different sermons preached on this parable, but the concept that Jehovah clearly blesses those who are wise and make an effort to improve upon the Divine favors they received is appropriate here. Here are seven key points to think about.

1. This implies their acknowledging that all their favours come from God. As long as men disregard the hand of the Giver, they will certainly despise His gifts.
2. A proper improvement of Divine favors implies a grateful sense of Divine goodness. The slothful servant did not thank his Master for the one talent.
3. A faithful improvement of Divine favors implies a cheerful and unreserved consecration of them to Him who gave them.
4. Faithfully improving Divine favors implies employing them in the service of God..
5. The faithful improvement of Divine favors affords the highest enjoyment of them. Men never enjoy their talents buried or abused.
6. The faithful improvement of Divine favors in time past prepares men for the reception of more and richer blessings in time to come. Masters bestow their best favors upon their best servants.
7. God's conduct confirms the declarations of His Word. He has in all ages bestowed peculiar advantages upon those who have improved the temporal and spiritual blessings He has given.

Action Plan -

Goal - What Divine Favors have you been entrusted with?

Why is this important to me?

What do I need to do to maximize what I have received?

When is my deadline?

Luke

DAY 23 - Luke 14:28

For which of you, desiring to build a tower, does not first sit down and count the cost, whether he has enough to complete it?

Meditation -

At first glance, it would be fair to suggest that this verse is simply telling us that in order to build wealth we need to have a plan. While I agree with this interpretation, I think the context of the verse has much deeper implications since the discussion is about discipleship.

When it comes to building wealth all of us first need to ask, what type of tower are we building? Will it be a colorful prism, a mere glass house made of material delights or a temple fortress in which we and Jehovah may dwell in harmony. As we develop our plans for financial freedom all us are unconsciously and consciously constructing up physical representations of our quest in the forms of cars, homes, stocks and other assets. However, we are also creating an environment for people to live, patterns for relationship and qualities of our character. As we build are we counting the cost of such decisions and actions? The answer is sometimes yes, then sometimes no.

While the prosperity of our business or financial endeavors have a place, they must not interrupt the formation of a pure and noble self. A self, which develops character qualities into the likeness of Jesus Christ. Building wealth requires a plan, resources to execute the plan and wisdom to make sure we are not giving up more than we are getting. The cost of an investment is not just the money to acquire the asset or the time it will take to develop the product, but it will also involve the moral decisions you will need to make a long the way.

Action Plan -

Goal - Have I considered all the sacrifices needed to accomplish my wealth building plan?
Why is this important to me?
What do I need to do to consider all?
When is my deadline?

DAY 24 - Luke 16:11

If then you have not been faithful in the unrighteous wealth, who will entrust to you the true riches?

Meditation -

Again, the Greek word "mamonas" or mammon appears. Here it is translated as wealth. The Parable of the dishonest manager offers us as stewards a lesson. The verse speaks to our stewardship of mere possessions and how faithfulness in the material world is reflective of our ability to be faithful to more important or "true" riches which are implied in the spiritual world. The challenge we face as followers of the Most High is managing wealth, riches, money, possessions or property with our future spiritual existence in mind.

The context strongly suggests that how we choose to manage our earthly wealth is a reflection of our heart. If we cannot be wise stewards of something as simple as wealth, how could we ever expect to manage more important things like people or our spiritual legacy?

Action Plan -

Goal - How do I want to handle true riches?

Why is this important to me?

What do I need to do to achieve my goal?

When is my deadline?

John

DAY 25 - John 10:10

The thief comes only to steal and kill and destroy. I came that they may have life and have it abundantly.

Meditation -

The words above were directly spoken by Jesus while he was speaking to the Pharisees in a parable. His parable was about "the good shepherd" and his sheep which he further explains is about himself and his followers. Jesus is directly stats that all others who have come before him were thieves. The Greek word used for thief describes a thief which steals in secret rather than in open violence.

The power in this verse is the comparison between the intent of the thief (to take and offer death) and the intent of Jesus (to offer both life and abundance). The Greek word for life is "zoe" which means both physical and spiritual life. The Greek word for abundance is "perissois" meaning abundance beyond what is anticipated or expected.

This verse is intended for all aspects of our lives. As it applies to our financial life, it is fair to surmise Jesus's intention is that both our physical and spiritual treasures are to be filled with abundance beyond our expectation. Are we expecting too little? Have we short changed ourselves and our shepherd because we do not fully understand the bigger spiritual picture of what Jesus has to offer us?

Action Plan -

Goal - To understand the abundant life God has for me:

Why is this important to me?

What do I need to do to achieve my goal?

When is my deadline?

DAY 26 - John 15:5

I am the vine; you are the branches. Whoever abides in me and I in him, he it is that bears much fruit, for apart from me you can do nothing.

Meditation -

These are again very direct words from Jesus, "Apart from me you can do nothing" especially for His Kingdom. Not unlike a grape vine, we are the small branches, which are dependent upon the main vine for nutrients and life. In order to achieve a lifestyle of abundance we must live in harmony with our life source, Jesus. Hence, the motto Live Faithfully, so that you can Live Abundantly.

Our role or responsibility is to make the choice to "abide" in Jesus. The word abide is a verb, an action word meaning to stay, dwell or remain. It is a word which describes a continual commitment of relationship with Jesus. The fruit of such a decision is first we please Jehovah. The second is a successful life filled with quality experiences and the creature comforts of daily living. By being in one spirit with Jesus we are now empowered to live a lifestyle of stewardship which will led to gains in all areas of life.

Building wealth is just one area of possibility. In this area, the manifestation of our relationship with Jesus will result in wisdom, spiritual intuition, opportunities, networking, divine appointments, doors being opened and doors being closed. It will led to having the energy to implement our wealth building plans and the wisdom to know when to rest and let Jehovah take over.

Action Plan -

Goal - How can I better abide in Jesus?

Why is this important to me?

What do I need to do to achieve my goal?

When is my deadline?

Romans

DAY 27 - Romans 13:8

Owe no one anything, except to love each other, for the one who loves another has fulfilled the law.

Meditation -

To really understand the full concept being presented in this verse, one must read it in the context of the chapter. The preceding verses discuss the importance of governing authorities, following their lead and paying our taxes to a system God has established for His service. Verse 7 sums up this concept of debt well, "Give to everyone what you owe them." The command begins with the material, taxes and revenue, but the Apostle Paul quickly elevates his discourse to how we deal with people. He encourages us to not be indebted to others with more important relationship characteristics like respect, honor and ultimately loving others.

The progression in these verses from the material, represented by money, to the emotional and spiritual, represented by love is where we find the lesson. If we weigh ourselves down with material debt we will never have time to be concerned with the more important spiritual things of life. With debt comes worry, enslavement, mental preoccupation with the burden of debt which for some of us can become all consuming. God wants our minds, and more importantly our hearts, to be focused on the spiritual aspects of living this life. He wants our behavior to focused on the service and love of others. He wants our daily experience to be about the quality of our relationships and not our ability to leverage material wealth.

Action Plan -

Goal - What debts do I need to settle?

Why is this important to me?

What do I need to do to achieve my goal?

When is my deadline?

2 Corinthians

DAY 28 - 2 Corinthians 8:9

For you know the grace of our Lord Jesus Christ, that though he was rich, yet for your sake he became poor, so that you by his poverty might become rich.

Meditation -

The sacrifice of ones self for the benefit of another is genuine Christian philanthropy. There are times when the act of dying to self requires the heart to bleed, hence the red heart. Within the context of chapter 8 we find three facts in relation to Christian philanthropy.

1. That true love for humanity is essentially associated with piety. Paul is speaking of the kindness which the church at Macedonia had shown to the sufferings of the mother-church at Jerusalem. The death sacrifice of Jesus which binds to God will also be the same glue which will bind the human race together.

2. That true love for humanity is an earnest element of character. These Macedonians seem to have been poor and afflicted, probably the subjects of persecution (ver. 2). However, their benevolence was not a mere act of sentiment, but a reaction to the compassion they had experienced in coming to know and follow Jesus. Their thought was simple, Jesus gave for us; therefore, it is only natural for us to give to others.

3. That true love for man has in Christianity the highest example, the death of one for the lives of many. Dying to self, this is genuine philanthropy.

Action Plan -

Goal - To fully understand what Jesus's death sacrifice means to me:

Why is this important to me?

What do I need to do to achieve my goal?

When is my deadline?

1 Timothy

DAY 29 - 1 Timothy 5:8

But if anyone does not provide for his relatives, and especially for members of his household, he has denied the faith and is worse than an unbeliever.

Meditation -
What can you say? The directive of this verse is clear, our financial provision for our family is to be our priority. We are to first make sure the financial needs and responsibilities of our nucleus family are taken care of. This would be for both immediate and future financial needs. Yes, we must be thinking about our financial legacy.

We are then to expand this practice to our extended family members and of course, this is much easier said than done. To be honest here, there will be those who do not want our help; and then there will be others who will want us to carry all their financial responsibilities. Neither extreme is healthy for the tribe; however, as leaders of the family we need to establish a pattern of living out our faith in a way which communicates to the tribe that we work together for betterment of the tribe.

Conclusion, wealth building is a family endeavor.

Action Plan -
Goal - to sit down with my immediate family and discuss the financial health of the family:

Why is this important to me?

What do I need to do to achieve my goal?

When is my deadline?

DAY 30 - 1 Timothy 6:17

As for the rich in this present age, charge them not to be haughty, nor to set their hopes on the uncertainty of riches, but on God, who richly provides us with everything to enjoy.

Meditation -

I was in a church elder meeting many years ago and there was a discussion about giving, church budget and stewardship. During the discussion one of the elders made a statement I had never heard before which was the "God gives to some the burden of wealth." At 27 I thought to myself, how is that a burden? God could give me that burden to bear. Clearly as a young man I had much to learn.

We all want to achieve financial independence, but we all are susceptible to placing our security in the wealth we have acquired. The Jehovah's word warns against placing our security into something which is uncertain. Money, real estate, stocks, commodities and other assets all have a degree of risk and uncertainty associated with them. Our misplacement of trust in what we have acquired can easily result in pride. When factors beyond our control change the value of the assets we have placed our security in our lives can quickly change as well and our security vanish over night. The only thing certain in this life is Jehovah Himself. He has to be the source of our security and trust.

Action Plan -

Goal - What is really my source of trust and security?

Why is this important to me?

What do I need to do to really test this question of myself?

When is my deadline?

Christopher Brown - started his writing career back in 2006 when he began contributing articles to the *Long Beach Journal, L.A. Times* and *Variety.* This side hobby evolved into becoming a regular contributor for an online publication called *The Power Player Lifestyle* magazine. In 2012, he published his first book entitled *Financial Crisis or Faith?*.

This first book inspired him to create a Christian personal finance non-profit called FaithFinance. As the Executive Director, Christopher is committed to building a community of believers who desire to live a lifestyle of stewardship. As a certified personal Financial Coach, he is driven to encouraging, educating and empowering others to "Live Faithfully, so that they can Live Abundantly."

Christopher Brown is on the board of directors for a non-profit Christian ministry called Restored Hope, Inc and is a member of Cottonwood Church in Los Alamitos, California. Professionally, he is a licensed architect, interior designer and construction project manager in California with a bachelor's degree in architecture from California Polytechnic University, San Luis Obispo. Being recently remarried, and a father of four, Christopher strongly believes his greatest accomplishment is having those closest to him know they are loved by him. As a native Southern Californian, Christopher loves the warm sun and the beautiful California coastline ... it is where he replenishes his soul.

Lightning Source UK Ltd.
Milton Keynes UK
UKHW020340270521
384421UK00007B/121